Selected from Life on Earth

David Attenborough

Supplementary material by Peter Zahler

and the staff of
Literacy Volunteers of New York City

OurWorld™

Readers House

LITERACY VOLUNTEERS OF NEW YORK CITY

OurWorld™ was made possible by grants from an anonymous foundation; Exxon Corporation; Scripps Howard Foundation; and H. W. Wilson Foundation.

ATTENTION READERS: We would like to hear what you think about our books. Please send your comments or suggestions to:

The Editors
Literacy Volunteers of New York City
121 Avenue of the Americas
New York, NY 10013

Selection: From *Life on Earth* by David Attenborough. Copyright © 1979 by David Attenborough Productions Ltd. Reprinted by permission of Little, Brown and Company. Supplementary materials © 1993 by Readers House, the publishing division of Literacy Volunteers of New York City Inc. Photos: p. 6 (top and bottom) © San Diego Zoo; p. 15 (top) Ron Garrison, © San Diego Zoo, (bottom) Ken Kelley, © San Diego Zoo.

Printed in the United States of America.

99 98 97 96 95 94 93   10 9 8 7 6 5 4 3 2 1

First LVNYC Printing: August 1993
ISBN 1-56853-002-1

OurWorld is a series of books published by Readers House, the publishing division of Literacy Volunteers of New York City Inc., 121 Avenue of the Americas, New York, NY 10013. The word "OurWorld" is a trademark of Readers House/Literacy Volunteers of New York City.

READERS HOUSE and colophon are trademarks of Literacy Volunteers of New York City.

Cover designed by Kevin Barry; interior designed by Jules Perlmutter/Off-Broadway Graphics.

Executive Director, LVNYC: Lilliam Barrios-Paoli
Publishing Director, LVNYC: Nancy McCord
Managing Editor: Sarah Kirshner
Publishing Coordinator: Yvette Martinez-Gonzalez
Marketing and Production Manager: Elizabeth Bluemle

Our thanks to the LVNYC Board of Directors' Publishing Committee: James E. Galton, Geraldine E. Rhoads, Arnold Schaab, Martin Singerman and James Stanko.

LVNYC is an affiliate of Literacy Volunteers of America.

Acknowledgments

Literacy Volunteers of New York City gratefully acknowledges the generous support of the following foundations and corporations that made the publication of READERS HOUSE books possible: an anonymous foundation; Exxon Corporation; Scripps Howard Foundation; and H. W. Wilson Foundation.

This book could not have been realized without the kind and generous cooperation of the author, David Attenborough, and his publisher, Little, Brown and Company. Thanks to Becky Hemperley, Permissions Department.

We deeply appreciate the contributions of the following suppliers: Creative Graphics (text typesetting); Delta Corrugated Container (corrugated display); Domtar Industries (text stock); Horizon Paper Company (cover stock); Offset Paperback Manufacturers, A Bertelsmann Company (cover and text printing and binding); and Phototype Color Graphics (cover color separations.)

Thanks also to Joy M. Gannon and Claire Walsh of St. Martin's Press for producing this book; Marilyn Boutwell for her time devoted to searching for selections; Peter Zahler for his skill and diligence in the research and writing of the supplementary material for this book; and to Miriam V. Sarzin for her thoughtful copyediting and suggestions. Thanks also to Laurie Krusinski at the Photo Lab, San Diego Zoo, for her help in obtaining photos.

Our thanks to Kevin Barry for his inspired design of the covers of these books. Thanks also Jules Perlmutter for his sensitive design of the interior of this book. Thanks also to Lloyd Birmingham for his accomplished design of maps and illustrations.

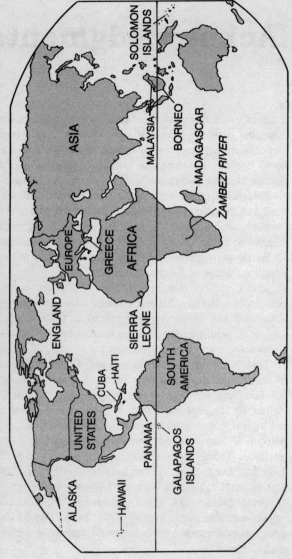

MAP OF PLACES MENTIONED IN THIS BOOK

ALASKA

HAWAII

UNITED STATES

CUBA

HAITI

ENGLAND

EUROPE

GREECE

AFRICA

ASIA

SOLOMON ISLANDS

MALAYSIA

BORNEO

MADAGASCAR

ZAMBEZI RIVER

SIERRA LEONE

PANAMA

GALAPAGOS ISLANDS

SOUTH AMERICA

Contents

Tamandua.

Pangolin.

Note
to the Reader

The study of animal life is called zoology. Zoologists are the scientists who study all aspects of animal life. They study how animals act, how their bodies work, how animals are related to each other, how animals are affected by their environment, how they affect their environment and how they evolved.

This series of books is called *OurWorld* because each book in the series tells you something about the physical world around you. Every book features the work of a well-known author who writes about science. Each book also tells you about the special area of science the writer studies. Knowing more about science may help you understand the things that shape the world as we know it. When you're reading this book, you may find some answers to questions you have had about our world and why it is the way it is. We hope you will want to explore and read about the many aspects that make up our world— past, present and future.

This book has different chapters. The Contents page lists these chapters and the pages where they start.

David Attenborough's writing is in the chapter,

"Selected from *Life on Earth*," starting on page 19.

Reading the other chapters in this book can help you understand David Attenborough's writing better, especially some of the scientific ideas that he is writing about. You may want to read some of these chapters before reading the selection or after reading the selection.

Here is what these chapters contain:

- The chapter, "About the Selection from *Life on Earth*," on page 12, gives you a preview of what you will read in David Attenborough's writing from *Life on Earth* that follows.

- In the selection from *Life on Earth*, there may be scientific terms or other words that are unfamiliar. In the Glossary on page 40, right after the selection, you can find the meaning of the words that appear in **bold** type in the selection. You may want to review the words in the Glossary to get familiar with them before you read the selection.

  In the selection, David Attenborough uses the British spelling for some words—like *specialised* rather than the American *specialized*. These words are in the Glossary as they are spelled in the selection, with the American spelling next to them in parentheses: ( ).

- The selection from *Life on Earth* is about zoology. The chapter, "About Zoology," on page 44, gives you more information about the history of this science and where it is today.

- The selection from *Life on Earth* talks about animals that are distantly related to each other. The chapter, "About Families of Animals," on page 46, gives you more information about how scientists group animals by common characteristics and how closely they are related.

- The selection from *Life on Earth* also talks about how some animals may have evolved from an earlier kind of animal and how they developed special ways to survive in different places. The chapter, "About Adaptation and Evolution," on page 52, gives you more information about the ways animals change over time.

- The chapter, "About David Attenborough," on page 57, tells you about David Attenborough's life. Sometimes knowing about a writer's life helps you understand his writing better.

- The chapter, "Questions and Activities for the Reader," on page 59, helps you build on what you have read. It has some ideas for group discussion and activities if you want to learn more about zoology. It also lists "Resources" on page 62, such as other books by David Attenborough and magazines and videos on zoology that can help you explore further.

- This book also has two maps of the world. One map, on pages 16 and 17, shows where the animals mentioned in the selection live; the other map, on the page facing the Contents page, shows all the places mentioned in the book. This book also has a "family tree," on page 18, of all the animals mentioned in the selection. There is a timeline on page 22 to help you understand when different groups of animals appeared on earth.

Reading about science will help you to be an *active* reader. Here are some things you can do.

Before reading, read the back cover of the book, think about its title and look at the picture on the front. Take a moment to think about why you want to read the book and what you already know about the science of zoology.

While reading, you will probably come across a word that is difficult to understand. You can find meanings for all the scientific words used in the selection in the Glossary on page 40. Reviewing these words may help you understand the scientific language used in the selection better. Think about what you are reading and ask yourself questions such as: Does this information support what I already know about zoology? or How can I use this information to answer questions I have about the science of zoology?

After reading the selection and some of the other chapters, try some of the questions and activities in the chapter on page 59. They are meant to help you discover more about what you have read and how it relates to you. The editors of *OurWorld* hope you will write to us. We want to know what you think about our books.

About the Selection from
Life on Earth

The tree shrew, the anteater, the bat, the whale—these animals differ from each other in size, shape and habits. They live in different parts of the world. But in some ways these animals are alike. This selection from *Life on Earth* tells about what such different animals can have in common.

David Attenborough wrote *Life on Earth* in 1979. Attenborough had created a popular series for British television called *Life on Earth* that was later brought to America. The TV show inspired him to write the book. The program showed the wonderful variety of plants and animals on the planet. The show helped viewers understand the evolution of life—that is, the way living things change over generations so they can survive better in their environments.

Life on Earth traces the development of life from the earliest known time to the present. Attenborough discusses the evolution of plant and animal life. He talks about the different groups of plants, insects, fish, reptiles, birds and animals.

This selection from *Life on Earth* focuses on one class of animals: mammals. Mammals are animals that share some special characteristics including having some body hair and producing milk for their young. Human beings are mammals. One of the ways animals within the mammal class are grouped is by what foods they eat in common: insects, plants, meat or all three. Most of the mammals discussed in this selection eat insects for their food. (Whales and dolphins are the exceptions.)

Attenborough begins by talking about the tupaia, or tree shrew, an animal that has fascinated scientists because they can't decide which order of mammals it belongs to. (An order is a large group of living things with common characteristics.) Attenborough tells how the first early mammal may have looked very much like the tupaia. These early mammals may have evolved into all the different mammals we know today.

He describes other unusual insect-eating mammals that live today, like the moon rat, the otter shrew, the solenodon and the tenrec. Others are more common, like hedgehogs, shrews and moles.

He tells how some insect-eating animals developed special features. The pangolin, the armadillo and the anteater all have long, sticky tongues to capture ants for food. Bats developed their wings in order to catch and eat flying insects, and a navigational system so they could catch them at night.

Whales and dolphins may have descended from a tiny mammal like the tupaia, and evolved to become totally adapted to, or changed in order to survive, life in the sea. Some whales have grown to be the largest mammals on earth.

The mammals Attenborough describes are pictured on the map on pages 16 and 17, which shows where they live. What can you tell about each animal's characteristics by looking at its picture? Before you begin reading, look at the pictures. In what ways are the animals different? How are they alike?

This selection from *Life on Earth* includes many words from the science of zoology. You can find their definitions in the Glossary on page 40.

Tenrec.

Hedgehog.

15

MAP OF ANIMAL HABITATS

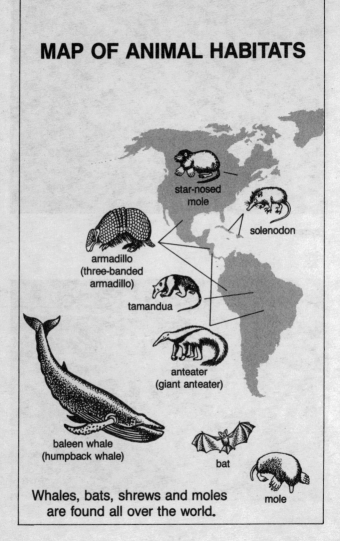

star-nosed mole

solenodon

armadillo
(three-banded
armadillo)

tamandua

anteater
(giant anteater)

baleen whale
(humpback whale)

bat

mole

Whales, bats, shrews and moles
are found all over the world.

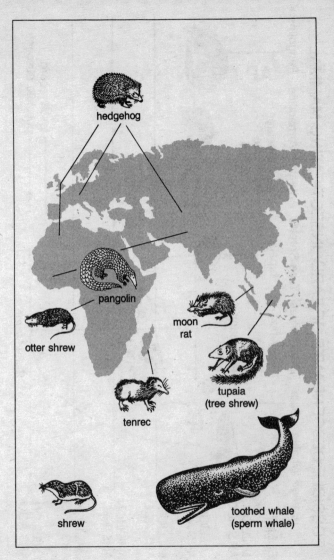

hedgehog

pangolin

otter shrew

moon
rat

tenrec

tupaia
(tree shrew)

shrew

toothed whale
(sperm whale)

17

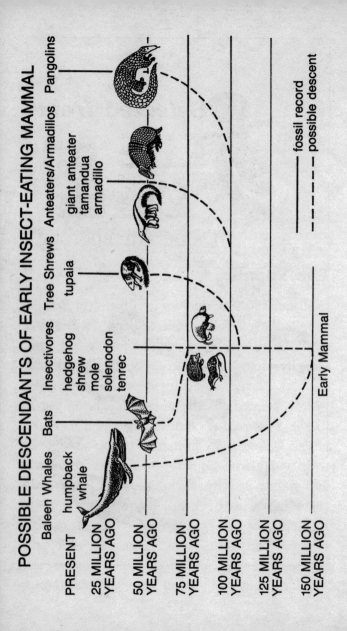

POSSIBLE DESCENDANTS OF EARLY INSECT-EATING MAMMAL

Baleen Whales	Bats	Insectivores	Tree Shrews	Anteaters/Armadillos	Pangolins
humpback whale		hedgehog shrew mole solenodon tenrec	tupaia	giant anteater tamandua armadillo	

PRESENT

25 MILLION YEARS AGO

50 MILLION YEARS AGO

75 MILLION YEARS AGO

100 MILLION YEARS AGO

125 MILLION YEARS AGO

150 MILLION YEARS AGO

Early Mammal

——— fossil record
- - - - possible descent

Selected from

Life on Earth

David Attenborough

The Tupaia

Sit quiet and motionless in a forest in Borneo and you have a fair chance of being visited by a small, furry, long-tailed creature which runs four-footedly along the branches of the bushes and over the ground, inquisitively testing everything with its pointed nose. It looks and behaves rather like a squirrel. A sudden unexpected noise makes it freeze, its glittering button-sized eyes wide with alarm. Equally suddenly it jerks back into frantic activity, flicking its tail backwards and forwards as it moves. But if, when it finds something to eat, it does not nibble at it with its front teeth but opens its mouth wide and champs vigorously with huge relish, then you are watching something much more unusual than a

19

squirrel and a creature of considerable significance—a tupaia.

If ever there were a creature that has been all things to all men, this is it. Local people in Borneo very understandably, regard it as a kind of squirrel; they use the word, *tupai*, which science has adopted, for all such animals. The first European scientists to catch a specimen, discovering that it lacked the gnawing teeth of a **rodent** and had numerous small spiky ones, called it a tree shrew. Other people believed that some details of its **genitals** indicated a relationship with **marsupials**. Half a century ago, a very eminent **anatomist** analysed the structure of its skull in great detail, noted that the creature had a surprisingly large brain, and argued that it should be regarded as an ancestor of monkeys and apes and classified it with them.

The debate is not over yet. Currently the balance of opinion has swung away from viewing it as an ancestral monkey and favours placing it with the shrews, but the fact that elements of so many different kinds of **mammals** can be seen in it, suggests that it might well resemble the ancient creature from which all **placental** mammals are descended. Certainly, judging from

fossil skeletons, the first mammals that scampered about in the **dinosaur**-dominated forests must have looked very like it—small, long-tailed and pointed-nosed, and, by inference, furry, **warm-blooded**, active and insect-eating.

The First Mammals

The reign of the **reptiles** had been a long one. They had come to power about 250 million years ago. They had browsed the forests and munched the lush vegetation of the swamps. Meat-eating forms had developed and preyed on the plant-eaters. Other **species** lived by scavenging carrion. The **plesiosaurs** and **ichthyosaurs** cruised the seas seeking fish; and **pterosaurs** glided through the skies. And then, 65 million years ago, all these creatures disappeared.

The forests of the world lay tranquil. No great beasts of any kind crashed their way through them. But in the undergrowth those small tupaia-like mammals, that had been there when the dinosaurs first appeared, still hunted for insects. That scene scarcely altered for hundreds of thousands of years. On a human time scale, such a period seems an eternity. Geologically it was only a moment. In the history of **evolution**, it was a phase packed with swift and dazzling invention, for during it the little **insectivores** produced descendants to fill all the niches vacated by the ruling reptiles and so founded all the great mammalian groups.

Timeline for Selection from *Life on Earth*

PRESENT

14 MILLION YEARS AGO	Human beings appeared.
50 MILLION YEARS AGO	Bats (flying mammals) appeared.
63 MILLION YEARS AGO	Mammals started to spread around the world.
65 MILLION YEARS AGO	Dinosaurs died out.
100 MILLION YEARS AGO	Birds appeared.
200 MILLION YEARS AGO	Pterosaurs (flying reptiles) appeared.
225 MILLION YEARS AGO	The first mammals appeared.
250 MILLION YEARS AGO	Dinosaurs appeared.
300 MILLION YEARS AGO	Flying insects appeared.

Other Primitive Insect-eating Mammals

Tupaia is only one of the primitive insect-eating mammals to have survived until today. There are others scattered around the world in odd corners. Many have misleading names that indicate how puzzled people have been about their true nature. In Malaysia, alongside tupaia, lives an unkempt irritable creature with a long nose bristling with whiskers and smelling powerfully of rotten garlic that is known, quite unaccountably, as a moon rat. In Africa there is the biggest of all which, because it swims, is called an otter shrew; and a whole group the size of rats which hop, have slender elegant legs and mobile thin trunks and which are known as elephant shrews. Cuba had a creature called a solenodon, though no one has seen a living specimen since 1909 and it may by now be **extinct**. Another solenodon species still flourishes in the neighbouring island of Haiti. And Madagascar has a whole group, some striped and hairy, some with spines on their backs, called tenrecs.

But all are not rare or restricted in distribution. That common inhabitant of the European countryside, the hedgehog, is also a primitive insectivore and is not so dissimilar from the rest if, in our mind's eye, we can discount its coat of spines. These are no more than modified hairs and are little indication of true ancestry. And there are also shrews. In many parts of the world they are very abundant indeed, scurrying through the leaf litter in hedgerows and woodlands seemingly always in a fever of excitement. Although they are only 8 cms [3 inches] from nose to tail they are very ferocious, attacking any small creature they encounter including one another. To sustain themselves, they have to eat great quantities of earthworms and insects every day. Among them is one of the smallest of all mammals, the pigmy shrew that is so minute that it can squeeze down tunnels no wider than a pencil. Shrews communicate with one another by shrill high-pitched squeaks. They also produce noises of a **frequency** that is far above the range of our ears, their eyesight is very poor and there is some indication that they use these **ultrasounds** as a simple form of **echo-location**.

The Moles

The shrew group has produced a **variant** that seeks its prey entirely underground, the mole. Judging from the structure of its paddle-shaped forelegs and powerful shoulders, it seems that the mole's ancestors were once water-living shrews and the mole has simply adapted the same sort of actions for moving along its tunnels. Fur, underground, might be thought to be something of a mechanical handicap, but many moles live in temperate areas and they need fur to keep warm. So it has become very short and without any particular grain so that it points in all directions and the animal can move forwards or backwards along its tight tunnels with equal ease. Eyes are of very little value underground. Even if there were any light to see by, they would easily clog with mud, so they are much reduced in size. Nonetheless, a mole must have some way of finding its **prey** and it has sense organs at each end. At the front, its main sensor is not its eyes but its nose which is an organ of both smell and touch, being covered with many sensory bristles. At the rear, it has a short stumpy tail also covered with bristles which make it aware of what is happening behind it. The star-nosed mole of America has an additional device, an elegant rosette of fleshy feelers around its nose which it can expand or retract.

Insect-eaters with Special Features

A few insectivores **specialised** early in eating one particular kind of **invertebrate**, ants and termites. There is no doubt as to what is the best tool for this job—a long, sticky tongue. The most extreme version of such a tongue is that evolved by the early placental mammals.

The Pangolins

In Africa and Asia, there are seven different kinds of pangolin, medium-sized creatures a metre [1 yard] or so long with short legs and long stout **prehensile** tails. The biggest of them has a tongue that can extend 40 cms [16 inches] beyond its mouth. The sheath that houses it extends right down the front of the animal's chest and is actually connected with its **pelvis**. The pangolin has lost all its teeth and its lower jaw is reduced to twin slivers of bone. The ants and termites collected by the mucus on the tongue are swallowed and then mashed by the muscular movements of the stomach which is horny and sometimes contains pebbles to assist in the grinding process.

Without teeth and without any turn of speed, the pangolin has to be well protected. It has an armour of horny scales that overlap like shingles on a roof. At the slightest danger the animal tucks its head into its stomach and wraps itself into a ball with its muscular tail clasped tight around it.

South American Insect-eaters

South America has its own particular group of insect-eaters which became separated from the rest at a very early stage. Their ancestors were among those placental mammals that, sixty-three million years ago, migrated down from the north through Panama and mingled with the marsupials. However the land bridge did not, in this first instance, last for long. After a few million years, it became submerged beneath the sea. So once more the continent was cut off and its animals evolved in isolation. Eventually, contact was re-established and there was a second invasion from the north as a consequence of which many of the recently evolved South American creatures disappeared.

THE ARMADILLOS

But not all. The least specialised of the survivors are the armadillos. Like the pangolins, they are protected by armour and it is this that gives them their Spanish-derived name. It consists of a broad shield over the shoulders and another over the pelvis, with a varying number of half-rings over the middle of the back to give a little flexibility.

Armadillos eat insects, other invertebrates, carrion, and any small creatures, like lizards, that they manage to catch. Their standard method of seeking food is to dig. They all have an excellent sense of smell and when they detect something edible in the ground, they suddenly start excavating with manic speed, scattering earth in plumes behind them, their nose jammed into the soil as though they are terrified of losing the scent and frantic to get a mouthful of food as soon as they possibly can. When you watch them, you wonder how they can possibly breathe. In fact they don't. They have the amazing ability to hold their breath for up to six minutes, even while digging. All armadillos have teeth.

THE ANT-EATERS

The specialist ant-eaters of South America, however, like the pangolins of Africa, have lost their teeth entirely. There are three of them. The smallest, the pygmy ant-eater lives entirely in trees and exclusively on termites. It is about the size of a squirrel with soft golden fur and curving jaws which form a short tube. A bigger version, the tamandua is cat-sized, has a prehensile tail and short coarse fur. It too is a tree-dweller but it often comes down to the ground. Out on the open plains, where termite hills stand as thick as tombstones in a graveyard, lives the biggest of the trio, the giant ant-eater. It is 2 metres [6 feet] or so long. Its tail is huge, shaggy and flag-like and waves in the breeze as the animal shambles over the savannahs. Its forelegs are bowed, and its claws so long that it has to tuck them inwards and walk on the sides of its feet. With these claws it can tear open termite hills as though they were made of paper. Its toothless jaws form a tube even longer than its forelegs. When it feeds, its huge thong of a tongue flicks in and out of its tiny mouth with great rapidity and runs deep into the galleries of the excavated termite hill.

The Bats

The insects first took to the air some 300 million years ago and had it to themselves until the arrival of the flying reptiles like the pterosaurs, some hundred million years later. Whether the reptiles flew at night we do not know, but it seems unlikely bearing in mind the reptilian problem of maintaining body temperature. Birds eventually succeeded them, but there is no reason to suppose that there were any more night-

flying birds in the past then there are today—
which is very few. So a great feast of nocturnal
insects awaited any creature that could master
the technique of flying in the dark. Yet another
variation of the insectivore theme managed to do
so.

That development took place very early, for
fossils of fully developed bats have been found
that date back to fifty million years ago.

The bat's flying **membrane** stretches not just
from the wrist, but along the extended second
finger. The other two fingers form struts ex-
tending back to the trailing edge. Only the thumb
remains free and small. This retains its nail and
the bat uses it in its **toilet** and to help it clamber
about its roost. A keel has developed on its chest
bone which serves as an attachment for the muscles which flap the wings.

The bats have many of the modifications developed by birds in order to save body weight.
The bones in the tail are thinned to mere straws
to support the flying membrane or have been lost
altogether. Though they have not lost their teeth,
their heads are short and often snub-nosed and so
avoid being nose-heavy in the air. They had one

problem that birds did not face. Their mammalian ancestors had perfected the technique of
nourishing their young internally by means of a
placenta. The evolutionary clock can seldom be
put back and no bat has reverted to egg-laying.
The female bat must therefore fly with the heavy
load of her developing **foetus** within her. In consequence, it is not surprising to find that bat
twins are a rarity and in almost every case, it is
usual for only one young to be born each season.
This, in turn, means that if the population is to
be maintained, the females must compensate by
breeding over a long period, and indeed, bats
are, for their size, surprisingly long-lived creatures, some having a life-expectancy of around
twenty years.

   Today, all bats fly at night and it is likely that
this was always the case, since the birds had already laid claim to the day. To do so, however,
the bats had to develop an efficient navigational
system. It is based on ultra-sounds like those
made by the shrews and almost certainly many
other primitive insectivores. The bats use them
for **sonar**, an extremely sophisticated method
of echo-location. This is similar in principle to

radar, but radar employs radio waves whereas sonar uses sound waves. These are of frequencies that lie a long way above the range of the human ear. Most of the sounds we hear have frequencies of around several hundred vibrations a second. Some of us, particularly when we are young, can with difficulty just distinguish sounds with a frequency of 20,000 vibrations a second. A bat, flying by sonar, uses sounds of between 50,000 and 200,000 vibrations a second. It sends out these sounds in short bursts, like clicks, twenty or thirty times every second and its hearing is so acute that from the echo each signal makes, the bat is able to judge the position not only of obstacles around it but of its prey which is also likely to be flying quite fast.

Most bats wait to receive the echo of one signal before emitting the next. The closer the bat is to an object, the shorter the time taken for the echo to come back, so the bat can increase the number of signals it sends the closer it gets to its prey and thus track it with increasing accuracy as it closes in for the kill. Not all bats feed on insects. Some have discovered that **nectar** and **pollen** are very nutritious, and refined their flying skills so that they can hover in front of flowers, just like humming birds, and gather nectar by probing deep into the blossoms with long thin tongues.

Other bats have taken to feeding on meat. Some prey on roosting birds, some take frogs and small lizards, one is reported to feed on other bats. An American species even manages to fish.

The vampire bat has become very specialised indeed. Its front teeth are modified into two triangular razors. It settles gently on a sleeping mammal, a cow or even a human being. Its saliva contains an **anti-coagulant**, so that the blood, when it appears, will continue to ooze for some time before a clot forms. The vampire then squats beside the wound lapping the blood. They fly by sonar and it is said that the reason that dogs, whose hearing is also tuned to very high frequencies, are so seldom attacked by them is that they can hear the vampires coming.

All in all there are nearly a thousand species of bats. They have made homes for themselves and found sufficient food in all but the very coldest parts of the world. The connection

between them and the tupaia pattern is not difficult to credit when you look at them closely.
They must be reckoned one of the most success-
ful of the early insectivore variations.

The Whales and Dolphins

Whales and dolphins, of course, are also
warm-blooded, milk-producing mammals and
they too have a long ancestry, with fossils dat-
ing back to the beginning of the great radiation
of the mammals [the spread of mammals all over
the world] fifty million years ago. But could
these immense animals really be descended from
a tiny creature like a tupaia? It is difficult to be-
lieve, and yet the logic of the deduction is unde-
niable. Their ancestors must have entered the sea
at a time when the only mammals in existence
were the little insectivores. But their anatomy is
now so extremely adapted to swimming that it
gives no clue as to how the move into the sea
was made. It may be that the two main groups
of whales have different ancestries, those with
teeth having come from insectivores by way of

primitive **carnivores** and the rest, the **baleen** whales, being descended more directly.

The major differences between the whales and the early mammals are attributable to adaptations for the swimming life. The forelimbs have become paddles. The rear limbs have been lost altogether, though there are a few small bones buried deep in the whale's body to prove that the whale's ancestors really did, at one time, have back legs. Fur, that hallmark of the mammals, depends for its effect as an **insulator** on air trapped between the hairs. So it is of little use to a creature that never comes to dry land, and the whales have lost that too, though once again there are relics, a few bristles on the snout to demonstrate that they once had a coat. Insulation, however, is still needed and whales have developed blubber, a thick layer of fat beneath the skin that prevents their body heat from escaping even in the coldest seas.

The mammals' dependency on air for breathing must be considered a real handicap in water, but the whale has minimised the problem by breathing even more efficiently than most land-livers. Man only clears about 15% of the air in his lungs with a normal breath. The whale, in one of its roaring, spouting exhalations, gets rid of about 90% of its spent air. As a result it only has to take a breath at very long intervals. It also has in its muscles a particularly high concentration of a substance called myoglobin, that enables it to store oxygen. It is this constituent that gives whale meat its characteristic dark colour. With the help of these techniques, the fin-back whale, for example, can dive to a depth of 500 metres [1,640 feet] and swim for forty minutes without drawing breath.

One group of whales has specialised in feeding on tiny shrimp-like **crustaceans**, krill, which swarm in vast clouds in the sea. Just as teeth are of no value to mammals feeding on ants, so they are no use to those eating krill. So these whales, like ant-eaters, have lost their teeth. Instead they have baleen, sheets of horn, feathered at the edges, that hang down like stiff, parallel curtains from the roof of the mouth. The whale takes a huge mouthful of water in the middle of the shoal of krill, half-shuts its jaws and then expels the water by pressing its tongue forward so that the krill remains and can be swallowed. Sometimes it gathers the krill by slowly cruising where it is thickest. It also can concentrate a dispersed shoal by diving beneath it and then spiralling up, expelling bubbles as it goes, so that the krill is driven towards the centre of the spiral. Then the whale itself, jaws pointing upwards, rises in the centre and gathers them in one gulp.

On such a diet, the baleen whales have grown to an immense size. The blue whale, the biggest of all, grows to over 30 metres [98 feet] long and weighs as much as twenty-five bull elephants.

The toothed whales feed on different prey. The largest of them, the squid-eating sperm whale, only attains half the size of the blue whale. The smaller ones, dolphins, porpoises and killer whales, hunt both fish and squid and have become extremely fast swimmers, some reputedly being able to reach speeds of over 40 kph [24 mph].

The great whales also have voices. Humpbacks, one of the baleen whales, congregate every spring in Hawaii to give birth to their young and to mate. Some of them also sing. Their song consists of a sequence of yelps, growls, high-pitched squeals and long-drawn-out rumbles. And the whales declaim these songs hour after hour in extended stately recitals. They contain unchanging sequences of notes that have been called themes. Each theme may be repeated over and over again—the number of times varies but the order of the themes in a song is always the same in any one season.

We still do not know why whales sing. Man can identify each individual whale by its song and if he can do so, then surely whales can do the same. Water transmits sound better than air so it may well be that sections of these songs, particularly those low vibrating notes, can be heard by other whales ten, twenty, even thirty miles away informing them of the whereabouts and activities of the whole whale community.

Ant-eaters, bats, moles and whales—to such extremes have the descendants of those early protean insectivores gone in the search for their invertebrate food.

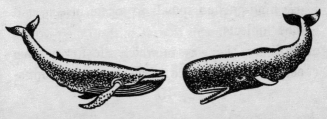

Glossary

anatomist. Someone who studies the structure or body parts of animals.

anti-coagulant. A substance that keeps blood from clotting.

baleen. A substance found along the upper jaws of some whales that strains food from the water.

carnivore. An animal that eats meat.

crustaceans. Animals that live in the water, have shells, three-part bodies, jointed legs and two pairs of antennae. Lobsters, shrimps and crabs are crustaceans.

dinosaurs. Large reptiles that lived on earth from about 250 million years ago until 65 million years ago. Dinosaurs are now extinct.

echo-location. Locating an object by measuring the time it takes an echo to return. Bats use high-pitched sounds to locate insects and other objects.

evolution. The way in which life forms have changed over time to produce new life forms.

extinct. A type of living thing is extinct when every one of its kind has died.

foetus (fetus). An unborn animal.

fossil. A plant or animal preserved over time in rock. Fossils tell us how early living things looked.

frequency. Sound waves can be given off at different frequencies. High-pitched sounds have higher frequencies than low-pitched sounds. Many animals can hear frequencies higher than people can.

genitals. The sexual organs of an animal.

ichthyosaurs. Extinct swimming reptiles with fishlike bodies.

insectivores. An order of small mammals, such as the tupaia, that eat insects.

insulator. Something through which heat or electricity does not pass easily.

invertebrate. An animal that does not have a backbone, such as an ant.

mammals. Animals that are warm-blooded vertebrates (having a backbone) that produce milk, breathe air and have hair.

marsupials. Non-placental mammals that carry their young in a belly pouch, such as kangaroos.

membrane. A thin sheet of plant or animal matter.

nectar. A sweet liquid made by certain plants.

pelvis. A large bowl-shaped bone structure of the hip area.

placental. Having to do with the *placenta*, an organ that provides a fetus with food, oxygen, and hormones and takes away waste products. Unborn placental mammals develop fully within their mother's uterus. Most mammals, including humans, are placental.

plesiosaurs. Extinct swimming reptiles with paddle-like limbs.

pollen. Tiny grains made by flowering plants that contain the male sex cells.

prehensile. Designed for grasping or climbing.

prey. An animal taken as food.

pterosaurs. Extinct flying reptiles.

reptiles. Cold-blooded vertebrates (animals with a backbone) that have dry, scaly skin. Because they are cold-blooded, the body temperatures of these animals go up and down with the outside temperature. Snakes are a kind of reptile; dinosaurs may have been reptiles.

rodent. An order of small mammals with two chisel-shaped front teeth. A squirrel is a type of rodent.

sonar. This stands for *so*und *na*vigation *r*anging. Sonar detects objects by timing the return of a sound pulse or echo.

specialised (specialized). Changed to adapt better.

species. A group of living things that can breed with each other.

toilet. The act of grooming.

ultra-sounds. Sound vibrations too high for humans to hear.

variant. One of two or more things that are slightly different.

warm-blooded. Mammals are warm-blooded. This means when the outside temperature goes up or down, their body temperatures remain about the same.

About Zoology

The word *biology* means "the study of life." The science of biology is divided into two different areas. The study of plant life is *botany*. The study of animal life is *zoology*.

Zoologists study all types of animals, from the simplest one-celled forms to apes and humans, and all aspects of animal life. A zoologist might specialize in one area such as:

physiology: the study of animal body parts;
behavior: the study of animal actions;
ecology: the relationships of animals with the environment;
taxonomy: the relationships between animals and how they evolved.

Each type of zoologist approaches the study of animals in a different way. A physiologist who studies an anteater, for example, might try to find out how the muscles of its tongue work to pick up ants. A behaviorist might look into how an anteater locates ant and termite mounds, and what it does after finding one. An ecologist might try to learn how the presence of an anteater in an area affects the numbers and survival rates of ants and termites. A taxonomist might look at the anteater's bone structure to see how it evolved and how closely it is related to a pangolin or a shrew.

One of the first zoologists was the Greek philosopher Aristotle, who lived from 384 to 322 B.C. He wrote about many different kinds of animals, describing their appearance and their actions. In the Middle Ages, many explorers wrote *bestiaries*, books describing the beasts they saw in their travels. These early zoologists often did not look too closely at the animals they saw. Some of these books include descriptions of unicorns and strange monsters that never actually existed.

After the invention of the microscope in the 1600s, scientists were able to learn more about animals. They could study their blood and internal tissues. Many encyclopedias of animal anatomy were published during the 17th and 18th centuries.

Since our earliest days, we have tried to understand the world around us, including the world's animal life. By doing so, we have begun to understand how we are a part of the natural world and part of the evolutionary process, too. By studying the natural world we can better understand ourselves.

About Families of Animals

When you look around you, how do you understand the things you see? One way to understand the world is to put what you see into groups. For example, two very basic groups are: things that are alive and things that are not. If you see a dog on a sidewalk by a car, it is easy to group those things. The dog is alive, but the car and the sidewalk are not.

Living things can be divided into two groups: animals and plants. Grass is a plant and a cat is an animal. Animals and plants can be further divided into groups that have characteristics in common.

When you see a dog, you know it belongs to the group of living things, to the living things that are animals and to the animals that are dogs. But do you know what other kinds of animals the dog is related to and why? Or what its earliest ancestors might have looked like?

To answer some of these questions, scientists arrange living things in groups. The groups are determined by the relationships of the living things to each other. The science of grouping living things and what each group should be named is called *taxonomy*.

Taxonomists study many things to determine an animal's group. They look at the animal's body parts. What kind of bones does the animal have? What kind of muscle? How does the animal digest food? To study an animal's evolution, a scientist might also look at particular fossils. Fossils show what the animal's ancestors were like. As animals evolve, their bodies might change in many ways.

There are seven major group levels in taxonomy: Kingdom, Phylum, Class, Order, Family, Genus and Species. Using these groups, you can describe any animal in the world. Kingdom is the largest group, species is the smallest. (The levels from Kingdom on down get more and more specific in defining the similarities between related animals.)

Because people from different countries speak different languages, they may have different names for the same kind of animal. Sometimes even people who speak the same language have different names for an animal. For example, the largest wild cat in the United States has several different names: mountain lion, puma, cougar, panther, catamount and screamer. These names are called common names. Taxonomists use one scientific name from the Latin language to describe a specific animal; the mountain lion's scientific name is *Felis concolor*. Every animal has one scientific name. In this way, taxonomists from different countries can share their knowledge and know they are each speaking about exactly the same animal.

The Bat

KINGDOM *Animalia* Animal
PHYLUM *Chordata* Has a backbone
CLASS *Mammalia* Mammal
ORDER *Chiroptera* Bats
FAMILY *Vespertilionidae* Common or Plain-nosed Bats
GENUS *Myotis* Group of bats having similar kinds and number of teeth
SPECIES *lucifugus* Little Brown Myotis or Little Brown Bat

If you wanted to describe a bat using taxonomy, you would start with the kingdom it belongs to. The two main kingdoms are plants and animals. The bat is in the animal kingdom.

Next, you would classify the bat according to its phylum. The bat is in the phylum *Chordata*, or vertebrates, animals that have a backbone. An animal without a backbone, like an earthworm, is an invertebrate.

Once you knew the bat's phylum, you would decide which class it belonged to. The bat is in the class of mammals. All mammals have hair and produce milk for their young. An animal like a lizard, that has a backbone but does not have hair or feed milk to its young, belongs to a different class of vertebrates—the reptiles.

Mammals are divided into different groups called orders. Bats are the only mammals that fly, so they have their own order called *Chiroptera*. (This word means "winged hand" in Latin.) Within the order of *Chiroptera*, there are 900 different types or species of bats. They are grouped into families according to similar features. The Little Brown Bat, for example, belongs to the family of common or plain-nosed bats: *Vespertilionidae*. Within that family, it belongs to the genus *Myotis*. The members of this genus are of different sizes, coloring and habitats, but they share some common characteristics, like the number and kinds of teeth they have. The Little Brown Bat is the species *lucifugus*.

Scientists might call an animal by all seven names, from kingdom to species. Usually, they use only two names—the genus and the species. So the Little Brown Bat is called *Myotis lucifugus*.

Fossils show us whether animals that are different species today evolved from the same species and so are related. For example, not very long ago, there was just one kind of doglike animal. Over time, this animal evolved and became different animals such as wolves and dogs. But, because they have the same ancestor, we know they are closely related.

You might think that a pigeon and a bat are closely related. They both have wings and can fly. But a taxonomist would see that a bat has hair and feeds its young with milk. In contrast, a pigeon has feathers. The taxonomist would say that bats are in the class of mammals while pigeons are in the class of birds. As strange as it might seem, a bat is more closely related to a wolf than it is to a bird.

Taxonomy is more than just naming things, or a way for scientists to understand each other. It is a science that helps us understand how all living things are related to each other.

About Adaptation and Evolution

Have you ever noticed how many different kinds of animals there are? And how different all the animals look? Even in a group of one kind of animal, every individual is just a little different from all the others. For example, if you have ever had a pet dog, you know that you can tell your pet from all the other dogs of the same breed.

Animals live in every corner of the world, from the cold North and South Poles to the hot deserts and even in the deepest oceans. Every animal has characteristics that help it to survive in its part of the world. A characteristic that develops over time to help an animal survive is called an adaptation. A bird's wing is an adaptation for moving in the air. A fish's fin is an adaptation for moving in the water.

Think of how an anteater is adapted for eating ants and termites. It has a long sticky tongue for catching insects. It has very strong front claws for tearing termite mounds. If one anteater has a stickier tongue or stronger claws than the other anteaters, this anteater has an advantage over all the other anteaters.

Even a small advantage may be important during bad times. When there is bad weather, there may not be many insects. Only the best adapted anteaters will survive. And only the best adapted anteaters will breed.

Sometimes different species of animals have similar adaptations. Pangolins and anteaters are totally different species that live in different parts of the world. But pangolins and anteaters both eat ants and termites. Since these two unrelated species eat the same food, they have evolved similar adaptations. Both species have a long snout and strong claws. Both have a long, sticky tongue. Neither pangolins nor anteaters have teeth. They do not need teeth to catch and eat the small, soft insects that make up their food.

When two animals of the same species mate, their young will have traits from both parents. But the young will be just a little different from their parents. In some ways *you* may look like your parents, but you do not look exactly like either of them.

Some animals inherit or develop differences that make it easier for them to stay alive. An animal may be able to run faster or hide better than other members of its species.

If an animal has a better chance of staying alive, it has a better chance of breeding and having more young than other members of the species. These young may have the same qualities that helped their parent stay alive. If they do, they have a better chance of growing up and having their own young than other members of the species.

After many generations, a quality that increases survival will become more common in the species. For example, if a certain coloring makes an animal less visible to a predator who wants to eat it, then the animals with that coloring will survive and pass on their coloring to their young and, after generations, most of the species might have that coloring. Over a long period of time the whole species will actually change. The changing of a species over time is called evolution. Evolution does not happen quickly. It can take thousands or even millions of years.

Charles Darwin was the man who formed the theory of evolution. During the 1830s, Darwin, an Englishman, sailed over much of the world and saw many different animals. Some of the animals in different places differed physically by only a little bit. These animals seemed to be closely related. For example, certain small birds he saw on the Galapagos Islands were only a little different from small birds on the mainland, but they *were* different. He wondered if, a long time ago, small birds flew from the mainland to the island and over time changed slightly from the birds on the mainland. He began to think about how these changes could have come about.

Darwin defined evolution with five ideas. The first was that every animal is a little different from every other animal. The second was that animals have more young than an area can support. The third was that these animals will compete with each other for food, space and mates. The fourth was that only the most fit animals will survive. The fifth was that the most fit animals will breed and pass on their qualities to their young.

In evolution, animals slowly change from one form into another. Often animals still have parts of their old form. For example, a long time ago the ancestors of whales walked on land and had hair. Over time, as the ancestors of whales spent more time in water, they lost their need for legs and fur. Today, whales have lost all their hair except for a few strands on their snouts. Because whales swim, their forelimbs have evolved into flippers and only a few leg bones remain.

Animals struggle to survive. And animals compete with each other. Animals that are better adapted will breed more often, and over time a species will evolve to have those adaptations. Animals come in so many shapes, sizes, and colors because of evolution.

About David Attenborough

David Attenborough was born in London, England, in 1926. After studying zoology at Cambridge University, he got a job in book publishing. Soon after, he began his long career at the British Broadcasting Company (BBC) based in London.

Attenborough's interest in natural history began when he was a young man. Beginning in 1954, when he was in his twenties, he was able to combine his love of nature with his television career when he filmed and studied the animals and people of Sierra Leone in Africa. This journey, along with later trips to places like Borneo, the Zambezi River and the Solomon Islands, were made into a BBC television series called *Zoo Quest*.

Attenborough worked for the BBC for 20 years. He was the director of programming when he left in 1972. Since then, he has created many nature series for the BBC, some of which have been shown on American television. He travels all over the world to make these programs, filming rare animals and exotic places. The TV programs usually focus on the evolution and preservation of life on our planet. He has written several books in addition to *Life on Earth* about these issues.

Attenborough is very concerned about the dangers facing the environment. As he says, "We can see that we ourselves are part of [the] natural world and are dependent on it, and that the natural world, since we have become the most powerful of all creatures, is now dependent upon us."

Explaining the natural world and helping to save it has won Attenborough many awards, including a British knighthood. By educating readers and viewers about life on earth, he hopes to make them aware of the need to preserve their world and all its inhabitants.

Questions and Activities
for the Reader

1. If you could talk to David Attenborough, what questions would you ask about his work? Think about how else you could find answers to these questions and talk about them with others.

2. Zoologists and people who write about zoology use special words to describe the things they study and write about. Some of these words are ones that you hear every day, like "animal," and others are more specialized and not very common, like "mammal." You can find many of these specialized scientific words in the Glossary on page 40.

   Do you use words in your work or hobby that are unique? Would others understand these words if you didn't explain them? Make a list of "special" words you use at work or in your other pursuits. How does your list compare with those of others?

3. Did reading the selection give you any ideas for your own writing? You might want to write about:

- all the living things you have observed in one place such as your neighborhood, a park or a pond.

- the differences and similarities between a domestic animal, such as a cat or dog or horse, and its wild relatives.

- how you might have to evolve to live on a different planet.

4. Sometimes you can more easily understand or remember scientific facts by performing a scientific exercise. Write down the names of some animals you think might be related. Using an encyclopedia or other reference book, make up a taxonomic chart for each animal. See how closely they are related or where they start to become different.

5. Think about the ways human beings have evolved over the ages. Consider various parts of your own body and how they are designed to help you survive. Some things to think about are:

   a. Why do you have a thumb that moves in a different direction from your other fingers?

   b. Why do you stand upright?

   c. Why do you have teeth that both cut and chew?

   You could check your ideas in a book about human evolution. You might also want to think about ways humans might evolve in the future to adapt to new changes in the environment, such as the warming or cooling of the world's climate.

6. There are many animals that have become rare or endangered, such as the panda, snow leopard and ivory-billed woodpecker. Choose one that interests you. In your local library, find out about the animal you have chosen. Why is its survival endangered? Some of these animals cannot survive if their environment is changed. Is that true of your animal? How is its environment being changed? Find out what is being done to save the animal. Jot down some ideas about what *you* can do to help save the animal. One organization to contact about saving endangered species is Wildlife Preservation Trust International, phone (215) 222-3634.

7. Most animals have adapted in special ways that help them survive in their environment. Read about one of the following environments: *prairie*, *marshland*, *mountain*, *ocean*, *rain forest*, *desert*. List the animals that live in the environment you have chosen. Keep in mind the special adaptations an animal might need for your environment. For example, an animal might have long legs for running because it lives on the prairie. Another might have developed thick fur to help it survive in the far north. Think about how those traits have helped the animal survive and how these same traits might endanger the animal in a different environment. Talk with someone who has chosen a different environment and see what animals you have in common and which ones are different.

Resources

Libraries and bookstores have sections of books on animals, nature and the environment. You can also learn more about animals and their habitats by visiting a local zoo or museum of natural history.

Other Books by David Attenborough

The Living Planet, 1986.
The Atlas of the Living World, 1989.
Trials of Life, 1991.

Videotapes

The Ascent of Man
Life on Earth (13 cassettes)
Nova (10 cassettes)
The Living Planet (12 cassettes)

Magazines

Audubon
Discover
National Geographic
Natural History
Smithsonian

Television Shows

Nova, on PBS.
National Geographic Explorer, on TBS Superstation.
Wildlife, on The Discovery Channel.

Four series of good books for all readers:

Writers' Voices—A multicultural, whole-language series of books offering selections from some of America's finest writers, along with background information, maps, glossaries, questions and activities and many more supplementary materials. Our list of authors includes: Amy Tan * Alex Haley * Alice Walker * Rudolfo Anaya * Louise Erdrich * Oscar Hijuelos * Maxine Hong Kingston * Gloria Naylor * Anne Tyler * Tom Wolfe * Mario Puzo * Avery Corman * Judith Krantz * Larry McMurtry * Mary Higgins Clark * Stephen King * Peter Benchley * Ray Bradbury * Sidney Sheldon * Maya Angelou * Jane Goodall * Mark Mathabane * Loretta Lynn * Katherine Jackson * Carol Burnett * Kareem Abdul-Jabbar * Ted Williams * Ahmad Rashad * Abigail Van Buren * Priscilla Presley * Paul Monette * Robert Fulghum * Bill Cosby * Lucille Clifton * Robert Bly * Robert Frost * Nikki Giovanni * Langston Hughes * Joy Harjo * Edna St. Vincent Millay * William Carlos Williams * Terrence McNally * Jules Feiffer * Alfred Uhry * Horton Foote * Marsha Norman * Lynne Alvarez * Lonne Elder III * ntozake shange * Neil Simon * August Wilson * Harvey Fierstein * Beth Henley * David Mamet * Arthur Miller and Spike Lee.

New Writers' Voices—A series of anthologies and individual narratives by talented new writers. Stories, poems and true-life experiences written by adult learners cover such topics as health, home and family, love, work, facing challenges, being in prison and remembering life in native countries. Many *New Writers' Voices* books contain photographs or illustrations.

Reference—A reference library for adult new readers and writers.

OurWorld—A series offering selections from works by well-known science writers, including David Attenborough, Thor Heyerdahl and Carl Sagan. Books include photographs, illustrations, related articles.

Write for our free complete catalog: Readers House/LVNYC, 121 Avenue of the Americas, New York, NY 10013